This book belongs to

_____

Share your thoughts, pictures, and stories about
this book on Instagram and Twitter!
#bigandsmallbook

To Mom and Dad,
A lot of this book comes from my love
for the outdoors, which comes from you.
Thank you! —BW

For my wonderfully curious and adventurous
nephews, Justin and Desmond,
with love. —LW

DRIFTWOOD TREE PRESS.

BIG AND SMALL, GOD MADE THEM ALL. TEXT Copyright © 2015 by Ben Wilder.
ILLUSTRATIONS copyright © 2015 by Laura Watson. All rights reserved. Printed in the
United States of America. No part of this book may be used or reproduced in any manner
whatsoever without written permission except in the case of brief quotations embodied
in critical articles or reviews. For information, address Driftwood Tree Press, 3915 East
Ridge Drive, Nashville, TN 37211.

benjaminwilder.com

Book design by Diana Wade

Wilder / Ben
    Big and Small, God Made Them All / Ben Wilder
    p. cm.
    ISBN 978-0-9909865-7-7

First Edition: January 2016

Big and Small, God Made Them All

Ben Wilder

Illustrations by Laura Watson

Big and Small, God Made Them All

From buzzing bees

to roaring seas,

He made the whale

and the snail,

Pinky toes

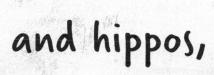

and hippos,

Icebergs

and hummingbirds.

He made the ox

and the fox.

He made a bat

and He made that.

He made a summer breeze

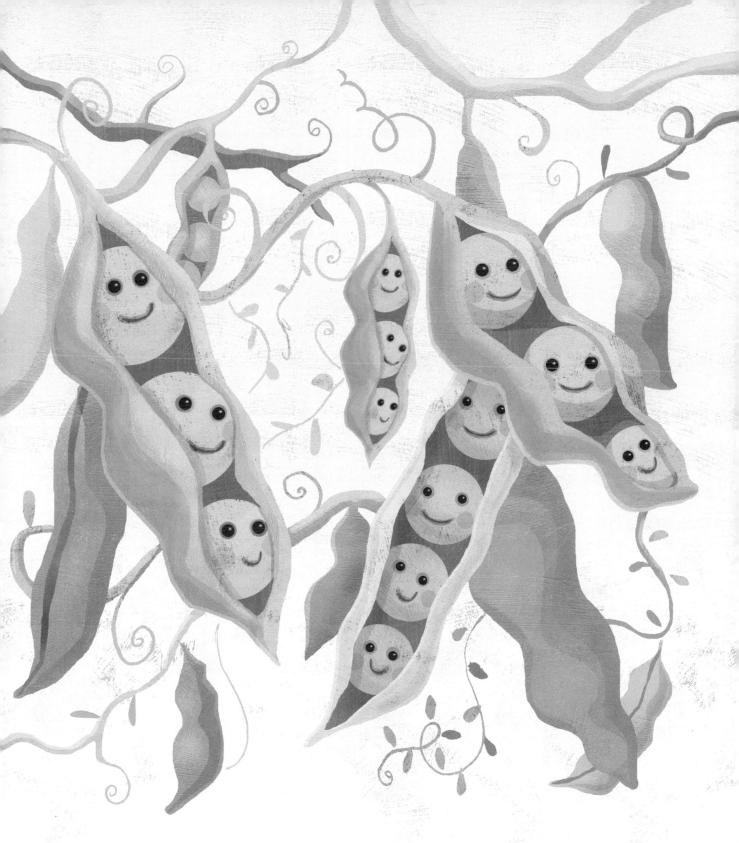

and green peas,

Potatoes

and volcanoes,

Dragonflies

and blue skies,

The moon.

and the raccoon,

Rainbows

and mosquitoes.

Yes, He made big things and small things, too.

But best of all,

He made YOU!